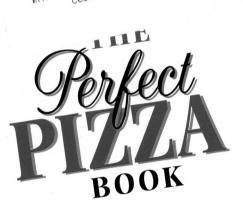

THE
Perfect
PIZZA
BOOK

C000202289

Photography by
Neil Sutherland

Food Stylist
Sue Michalski

Edited and Introduced by
Rosemary Moon

Design
Julie Smith

Production
Ruth Arthur, Neil Randles
Paul Randles, Karen Staff

Director of Production
Gerald Hughes

4891
This edition published 1997 by
Colour Library Direct
© 1997 CLB International
Godalming, Surrey, GU7 1XW
All rights reserved
Printed in Hong Kong
ISBN 1-85833-565-5

Contents

Introduction

Pizza – the original take-away

Is it true to say that pizza was the original fast food take-away and that it is as popular today as it has always been? This may be difficult to substantiate but a food very similar to the modern pizza was definitely a favourite of the people of Ancient Rome.

Although the Romans pioneered many of our 'modern' luxuries, for example central heating and the first bread ovens, such equipment was found only in the villas of the rich, and most people had nothing more at home than a pot over a fire for cooking. Trays of pizza look-alikes – sourdough bases spread with a basic topping and baked in market ovens – were cut up and sold for people to take home for their supper. It really is possible that pizza was the original take-away.

We now use a quick yeasted dough for a pizza base. Toppings vary from the basic Tomato & Cheese to Chicken with Thai Spices and American Hot. Indeed, many Americans might almost regard the modern pizza as their own invention, having introduced chillies and a variety of fruits and nuts to the more traditional Italian toppings.

Pizza is, without doubt, one of the most popular foods in the world, and is available just about everywhere. Accompanied by a tossed salad, it provides a healthy, well balanced and relatively low-fat meal.

Pizza-making at home

Personal preference will dictate whether you choose a thin crust or a deep-pan base. By experimenting with pizzas at home you have the start of an almost infinite culinary repertoire – potentially dull left-overs are enlivened with a basic tomato sauce, some seasonings and a little cheese. Don't be tempted to be too generous with your toppings – too much may prevent the base from cooking through properly. And don't worry about authenticity as so many foods around the world are eaten with bread to mop up the juices – a pizza is a basic meal, elegantly served. Left-over pizza also freezes well.

Both types of pizza base are quickly made using easy-blend dried yeast, but they benefit from at least 20 minutes proving to make a lighter crust. If possible, it is better to leave a deep-pan dough for 30-40 minutes before baking. The proving time can usefully be spent making the tomato sauce to spread over the pizza, or in preparing the other ingredients for the topping.

Keep a pack of ready-prepared pizza bases in the cupboard for those occasions when there is no time to make your own. These have a good flavour and quite dramatically reduce the cooking time, as well as the preparation time, of the finished pizza – 12-15 minutes in a hot oven is usually sufficient to heat the base through and cook the topping, although this will, of course, depend on the ingredients used.

In some pizza restaurants you may see pizza doughs being shaped and then baked immediately. These will have been made with a traditional fresh yeast dough that has already been allowed to rise for an hour or so. If you treat a quick dough in this way it will be very hard and cardboard-like when baked.

Savoury scone doughs may be used for pizza bases, but these can easily become too spongy in texture during baking, dominating the pizza and overpowering the topping. Bread bases definitely give the best results.

Italian cheeses for authenticity

Just a few years ago Mozzarella, Ricotta and many other Italian cheeses were only available in specialist food shops and delicatessens. The majority of supermarkets now carry a choice of buffalo or cow's milk Mozzarella (buffalo being the authentic but more expensive) and it is available ready grated or in 'pearls' – little balls ideal for cheese toppings.

Cheddar or other traditional English cheeses may also be used, or mixed with Mozzarella for economy. You may prefer the texture of melted Cheddar to the slightly stringy texture of Mozzarella. Some ingredients, especially oily fish such as sardines, benefit from a more pungent blue cheese like Gorgonzola.

Herbs for flavour

The recipes in this book use fresh herbs – do remember that you will only need half the quantity if using dried herbs. The most widely used herbs for pizzas are basil, oregano, marjoram and thyme.

Chicken, beef, sausages and salami, prawns and other shellfish all make excellent pizzas,but we probably think of pepperoni as the traditional pizza topping. This thin, spicy sausage is available whole, or ready cut into thin slices for convenience.

Pizza

Basic Thin Crust

This dough will produce a thin, crispy crust for your pizza. The addition of olive oil helps both the flavour and texture, and a 20 minute proving will give the dough sufficient time to start rising before adding the topping.

225g/8oz strong plain flour
1 tsp easy-blend dried yeast
½ tsp salt
1 tbsp olive oil
150ml/5 fl oz warm water (approx)

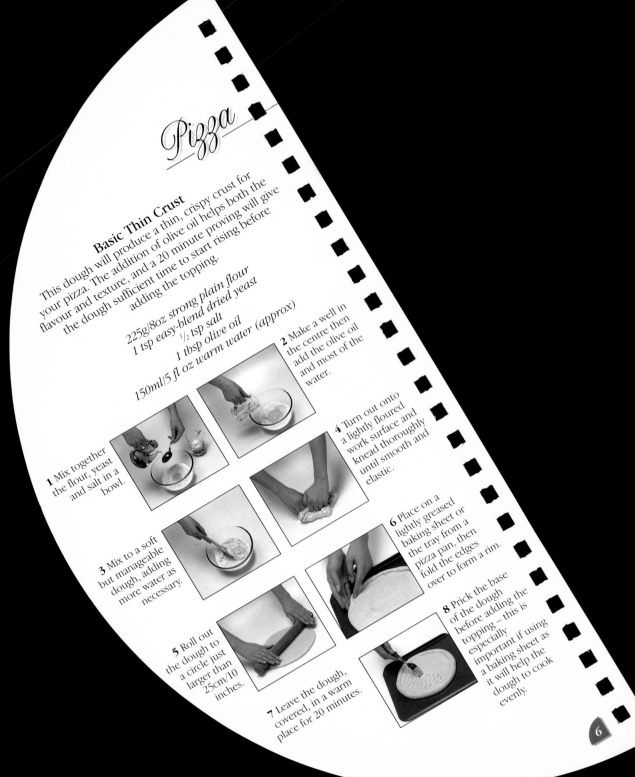

1 Mix together the flour, yeast and salt in a bowl.

2 Make a well in the centre then add the olive oil and most of the water.

3 Mix to a soft but manageable dough, adding more water as necessary.

4 Turn out onto a lightly floured work surface and knead thoroughly until smooth and elastic.

5 Roll out the dough to a circle just larger than 25cm/10 inches.

6 Place on a lightly greased baking sheet or the tray from a pizza pan, then fold the edges over to form a rim.

7 Leave the dough, covered, in a warm place for 20 minutes.

8 Prick the base of the dough before adding the topping – this is especially important if using a baking sheet as it will help the dough to cook evenly.

Bases

Deep Pan Base

This is a more traditional bread dough, soft and slightly spongy in texture. The method is the same as for the basic thin crust but the dough should be left for an extra 20 minutes in order to prove properly and produce the correct texture.

275g/10oz strong plain flour
1 tsp easy-blend dried yeast
½ tsp salt
175ml/6 fl oz warm water (approx)

Quick Tomato Sauce

Many pizzas have a tomato sauce spread over the dough to make a tasty base for the other topping ingredients. Use fresh tomatoes to make the sauce when they are plentiful, but canned tomatoes make an excellent quick alternative. This sauce is best made while the pizza base is proving.

2 tbsps olive oil
1 onion, finely chopped
1 clove garlic, crushed
200g can chopped tomatoes
1 tbsp freshly chopped mixed herbs
Salt and freshly ground black pepper

1 Heat the oil then add the onion and cook slowly until soft. Add the garlic with the tomatoes and herbs, then bring the sauce to the boil.

2 Simmer for 10 minutes, until slightly reduced and thickened. Season to taste with salt and pepper.

Pizza Rustica

This is a very filling pizza. The topping is deep
and combines ham, cheese and eggs with cream.
Build up a good edge on the dough or the
filling will escape.

M·E·T·H·O·D

1
Roll out the prepared dough as directed.

2
Cover the dough and leave in a warm place for 20 minutes, then prick the base thoroughly with a fork.

3
Preheat an oven to 220°C/425°F/Gas Mark 7.

4
Scatter the Parmesan over the pizza base and place the ham in a layer on top.

5
Cover the ham with the chopped tomato and hard-boiled egg.

6
Beat all the remaining ingredients together in a bowl, seasoning well.

7
Pour the filling over the pizza.

8
Bake in the preheated oven for 15 minutes.

9
Reduce the oven temperature to 190°C/375°F/Gas Mark 5 and cook for a further 15-20 minutes, until the filling is set and golden and the base is cooked through.

Pizza Rustica

I·N·G·R·E·D·I·E·N·T·S

1 quantity Pizza Dough of your choice

30g/1oz Parmesan cheese, freshly grated

3 slices Parma ham

2 tomatoes, skinned, seeded and roughly chopped

1 hard-boiled egg, chopped

2 large eggs, lightly beaten

60g/2oz Bel Paese cheese

60g/2oz Fontina or Gruyere cheese, grated

5 tbsps double cream

1 tbsp freshly chopped parsley

1 tbsp freshly chopped basil

Freshly grated nutmeg

Salt and freshly ground black pepper

MAKES: one 25cm/10-inch pizza
PREPARATION TIME: 35 minutes
COOKING TIME: 30-35 minutes

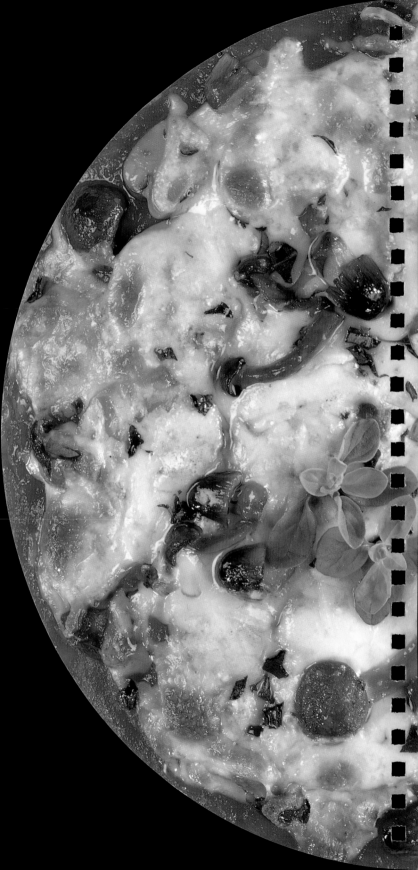

Mushroom Pizza

Use a variety of mushrooms, if possible, for this pizza – the oregano draws out their flavour and the combination of Mozzarella and Parmesan cheeses gives extra bite to the topping.

M·E·T·H·O·D

1

2
Cover the dough and
leave in a warm place for 20
minutes, then prick the
base thoroughly with a fork.
out the prepared
dough as directed.

3
Preheat an oven to
220°C/425°F/Gas Mark 7.

4
Heat 2 tbsps oil in a
saucepan, add the
mushrooms and cook
until soft, then stir in
the seasonings and
garlic.

5
Spread the pizza base
with tomato sauce,
then top with the
mushrooms.

6
Scatter the Mozzarella and
Parmesan over the pizza.

7
Drizzle the remaining
oil over the cheeses.

8
Bake in the preheated oven
for 20-25 minutes, until the
base is cooked and the
topping lightly browned.

Mushroom Pizza

I·N·G·R·E·D·I·E·N·T·S

1 quantity Pizza Dough of your choice

1 quantity Tomato Sauce

3 tbsps olive oil

120g/4oz mushrooms, sliced

2 tsps freshly chopped oregano

Salt and freshly ground black pepper

1 clove garlic, crushed

90g/3oz Mozzarella cheese, grated

30g/1oz Parmesan cheese, freshly grated

MAKES: one 25cm/10-inch pizza
PREPARATION TIME: 30 minutes
COOKING TIME: 20-25 minutes

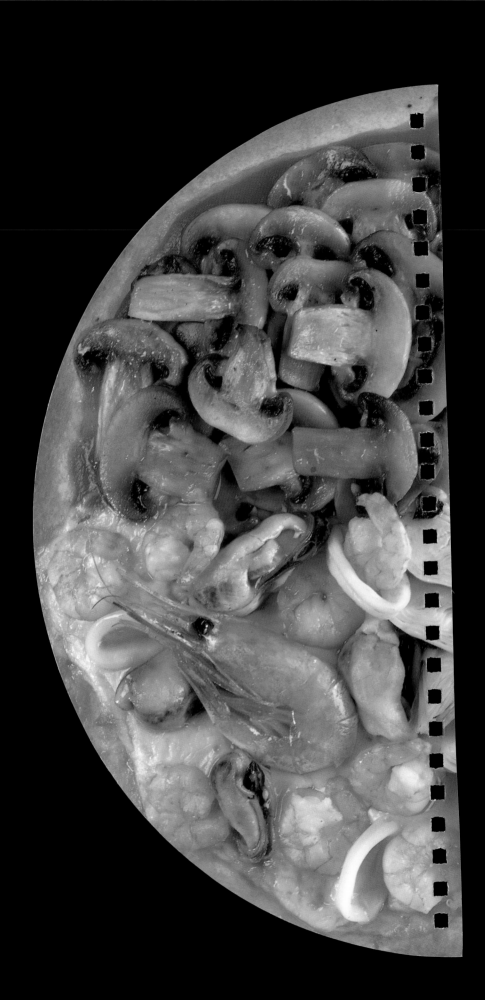

Four Seasons Pizza

Four toppings to represent four seasons – you could, of course, use four toppings of your own choice but select ingredients that vary in colour, taste and texture.

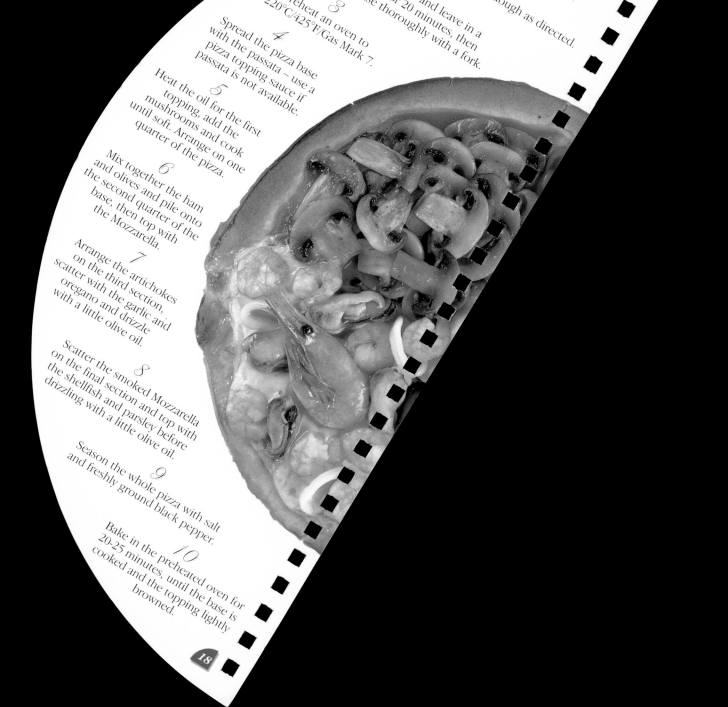

3
...heat an oven to 220°C/425°F/Gas Mark 7.

4
Spread the pizza base with the passata – use a pizza topping sauce if passata is not available.

5
Heat the oil for the first topping, add the mushrooms and cook until soft. Arrange on one quarter of the pizza.

6
Mix together the ham and olives and pile onto the second quarter of the base, then top with the Mozzarella.

7
Arrange the artichokes on the third section, scatter with the garlic and oregano and drizzle with a little olive oil.

8
Scatter the smoked Mozzarella on the final section and top with the shellfish and parsley before drizzling with a little olive oil.

9
Season the whole pizza with salt and freshly ground black pepper.

10
Bake in the preheated oven for 20-25 minutes, until the base is cooked and the topping lightly browned.

...and leave in a ...e thoroughly with a fork.

...r 20 minutes, then

...ough as directed.

18

Four Seasons Pizza

I·N·G·R·E·D·I·E·N·T·S

1 quantity Pizza Dough of your choice

4 tbsps passata

FIRST QUARTER

1 tbsp olive oil

60g/2oz mushrooms, sliced

SECOND QUARTER

1 slice Parma ham, cut into strips

2 black olives, pitted and chopped

30g/1oz Mozzarella cheese, grated

THIRD QUARTER

4 canned artichoke hearts, sliced

1 clove garlic, chopped or crushed

Pinch of freshly chopped oregano

Olive oil

FOURTH QUARTER

30g/1oz smoked or plain Mozzarella cheese, grated

90g/3oz mixed prepared shellfish

1 tsp freshly chopped parsley

Olive oil

Salt and freshly ground black pepper

MAKES: one 25cm/10-inch pizza
PREPARATION TIME: 30 minutes
COOKING TIME: 20-25 minutes

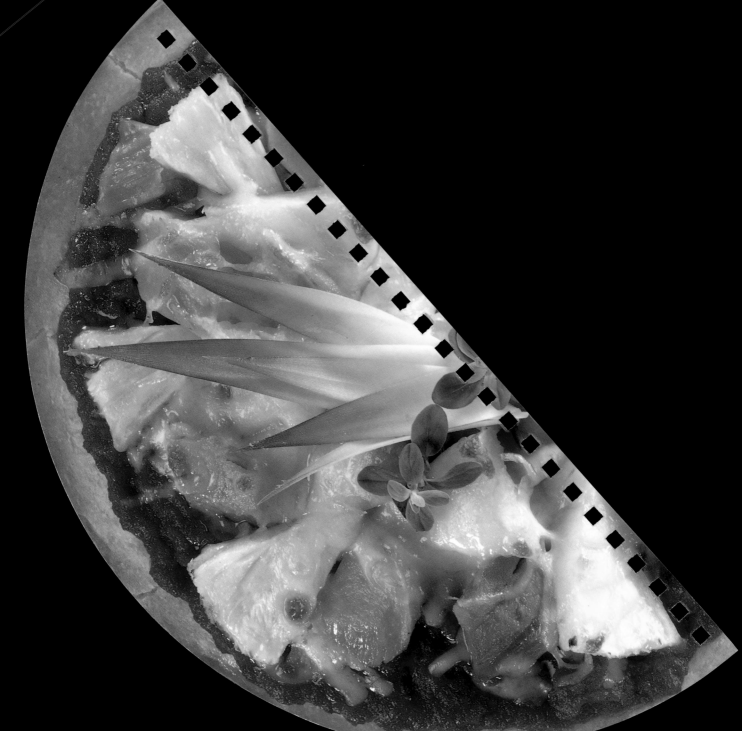

Pizza Tropicana

Although ham and pineapple may seem a strange classic combination for an Italian savoury, this topping is certainly one of the most popular in pizza restaurants.

M·E·T·H·O·D

1
Roll out the prepared
dough as directed.

2
Cover the dough and
leave in a warm place for
20 minutes, then prick the
base thoroughly with a fork.

3
Preheat an oven to
220°C/425°F/Gas Mark 7.

4
Mix the tomato sauce
with the allspice and
spread over the pizza base.

5
Arrange the ham and
pineapple over the sauce.

6
Season well then add
oregano to taste.

7
Scatter the Mozzarella
over the pizza.

8
Bake in the preheated oven
for 20-25 minutes, until the
base is cooked and the
topping lightly browned.

9
If the meats begin to brown too
quickly, cover the pizza with a
loose tent of cooking foil until
the base is cooked.

22

Pizza Tropicana

I·N·G·R·E·D·I·E·N·T·S

1 quantity Pizza Dough of your choice

1 quantity Tomato Sauce

Pinch of ground allspice

2 thick slices ham, diced

60g/2oz pineapple chunks, fresh or canned

Salt and freshly ground black pepper

Freshly chopped oregano

120g/4oz Mozzarella cheese, grated

MAKES: one 25cm/10-inch pizza
PREPARATION TIME: 30 minutes
COOKING TIME: 20-25 minutes

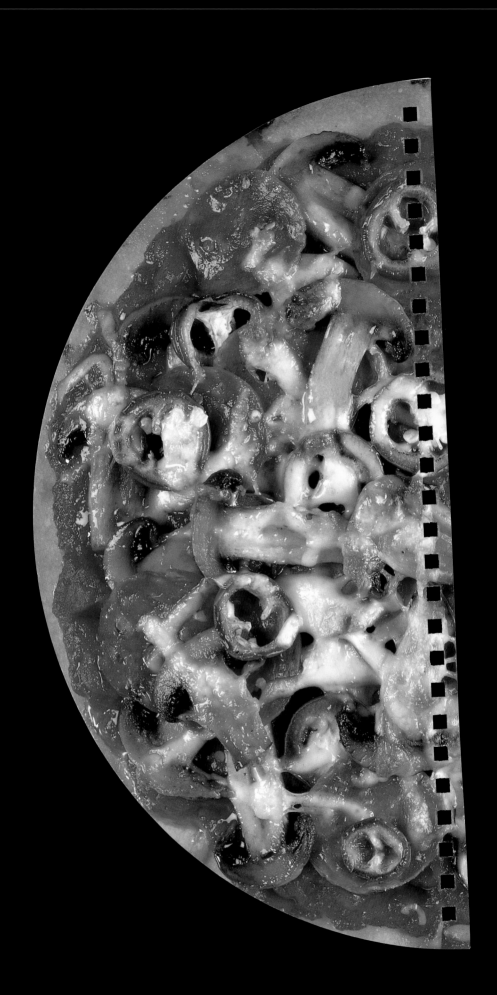

Pepperoni & Green Chilli Pizza

Sometimes known as 'American Hot' this pizza is not for the faint-hearted! The chillies are added complete with their seeds, although they may be removed for a milder flavour.

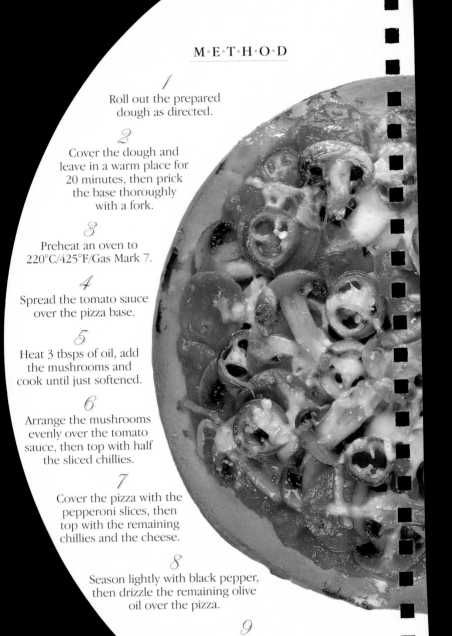

M·E·T·H·O·D

1
Roll out the prepared dough as directed.

2
Cover the dough and leave in a warm place for 20 minutes, then prick the base thoroughly with a fork.

3
Preheat an oven to 220°C/425°F/Gas Mark 7.

4
Spread the tomato sauce over the pizza base.

5
Heat 3 tbsps of oil, add the mushrooms and cook until just softened.

6
Arrange the mushrooms evenly over the tomato sauce, then top with half the sliced chillies.

7
Cover the pizza with the pepperoni slices, then top with the remaining chillies and the cheese.

8
Season lightly with black pepper, then drizzle the remaining olive oil over the pizza.

9
Bake in the preheated oven for 20-25 minutes, until the base is cooked and the topping lightly browned.

Pepperoni & Green Chilli Pizza

I·N·G·R·E·D·I·E·N·T·S

1 quantity Pizza Dough of your choice

1 quantity Tomato Sauce

4 tbsps olive oil

120g/4oz mushrooms, sliced

2 green chillies, sliced

60g/2oz pepperoni, finely sliced

120g/4oz Mozzarella cheese, sliced

Freshly ground black pepper

MAKES: one 25cm/10-inch pizza
PREPARATION TIME: 30 minutes
COOKING TIME: 20-25 minutes

27

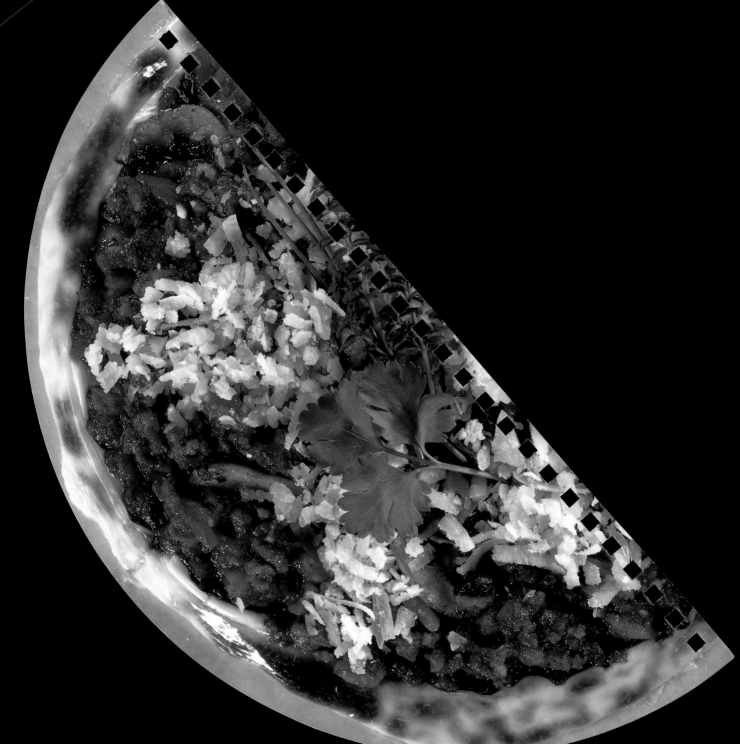

Bolognese-Topped Pizza

A rich meat sauce usually served with pasta, Bolognese is probably the most famous Italian dish. This is a quick Bolognese sauce, served as an unusual pizza topping.

M·E·T·H·O·D

1
Roll out the prepared
dough as directed.

2
Cover the dough and leave
in a warm place for 20-30
minutes, then prick the base
thoroughly with a fork.

3
Preheat an oven to
220°C/425°F/Gas Mark 7.

4
Heat the oil, add the
onion and cook until
starting to brown.

5
Add the minced beef
and garlic and cook
quickly until well
browned.

6
Stir in all the remaining
ingredients except the
cheeses, and simmer
for 10 minutes.
Season to taste.

7
Spread the Mascarpone
over the pizza base then
spoon the Bolognese
sauce over the top,
leaving a border of
the cheese.

8
Bake in the preheated oven for
20-25 minutes, until the base is
cooked and the topping lightly
browned.

9
Spoon the Parmesan over
the pizza just before serving.

Bolognese-topped Pizza

INGREDIENTS

1 quantity Pizza Dough of your choice

1 tbsp olive oil

1 small onion, sliced

225g/8oz lean minced beef

1 clove garlic, crushed

60g/2oz mushrooms, sliced

200g/7oz can chopped tomatoes

1 tbsp freshly chopped mixed herbs

1 tbsp tomato purée

Salt and freshly ground black pepper

3 tbsps Mascarpone cheese

30g/1oz Parmesan cheese, freshly grated

MAKES: one 25cm/10-inch pizza
PREPARATION TIME: 35 minutes
COOKING TIME: 20-25 minutes

Pizza Chicken Tikka

A curry topping for a pizza might seem an extraordinary idea, but the spiced chicken blends well with the tomato sauce and the pizza base is very similar to naan bread.

M·E·T·H·O·D

1

Mix together the yogurt, ginger, garlic, chilli, turmeric, coriander, salt, pepper, lemon juice and oil in a shallow dish.

2

Add the chicken pieces and turn them over in the marinade until well coated. Cover and leave to marinate in the refrigerator for at least 6 hours, or overnight.

3

Roll out the prepared dough as directed.

4

Cover the dough and leave in a warm place for 20 minutes, then prick the base thoroughly with a fork.

5

Preheat an oven to 220°C/425°F/Gas Mark 7.

6

Spread the tomato sauce over the pizza base and bake in the preheated oven for 10 minutes.

7

Remove the pizza from the oven and arrange the chicken pieces over the tomato sauce. Spoon the marinade over the chicken and scatter the pizza with the chopped pepper.

8

Bake the pizza for a further 15-20 minutes, until both the base and the chicken are cooked.

9

Serve garnished with coriander sprigs and lemon wedges.

Pizza Chicken Tikka

I·N·G·R·E·D·I·E·N·T·S

150ml/5 fl oz natural yogurt

2.5cm/1-inch piece root ginger, peeled and grated

1 clove garlic, crushed

1 tsp chilli powder

½ tsp ground turmeric

2 tsps ground coriander

Salt and freshly ground black pepper

1 tbsp lemon juice

2 tbsps sunflower oil

2 boneless chicken breasts, skinned and diced

1 quantity Pizza Dough of your choice

1 quantity Tomato Sauce

½ green pepper, seeded and chopped

Fresh coriander sprigs and lemon wedges to garnish

MAKES: one 25cm/10-inch pizza
PREPARATION TIME: 30 minutes plus marinating
COOKING TIME: 25-30 minutes

Chicken Pizza with Thai Spices

This certainly isn't a traditional pizza but the Thai spices combine well with the chicken to produce a delicious topping. Use Chinese five-spice powder if the Thai seven-spice powder is not available.

M·E·T·H·O·D

1
Roll out the prepared dough as directed.

2
Cover the dough and leave in a warm place for 20 minutes, then prick the base thoroughly with a fork.

3
Preheat an oven to 220°C/425°F/Gas Mark 7.

4
Spread the Tomato Sauce over the pizza base.

5
Heat the oil, add the pepper and cook until just softened. Remove with a draining spoon and set the pepper aside.

6
Add the mushrooms to the pan and cook for 2 minutes; remove and set aside.

7
Stir the seven-spice mixture into the pan and cook slowly for 1 minute, then add the chicken strips. Increase the heat and cook until the chicken begins to brown.

8
Return the mushrooms to the pan with the spring onions and mix well.

9
Scatter half the pepper over the Tomato Sauce then spread the chicken mixture over the pizza. Top with the remaining pepper and the sliced cheese.

10
Bake for 20-25 minutes, until the base is cooked and the topping lightly browned. Garnish with coriander.

Chicken _____ with Thai Spice

I·N·G·R·E·D·I·E·N·T·S

1 quantity Pizza Dough of your choice

1 quantity Tomato Sauce

2 tbsps peanut or sunflower oil

½ yellow pepper, seeded and chopped

60g/2oz mushrooms, sliced

2 tsps Thai seven-spice powder

1 boneless chicken breast, skinned and cut into strips

1 bunch spring onions, trimmed and cut into 2.5cm/1-inch lengths

90g/3oz Mozzarella cheese, sliced

Fresh coriander sprigs to garnish

MAKES one 25cm/10-inch pizza
PREPARATION TIME: 40 minutes
COOKING TIME: 20-25 minutes

39

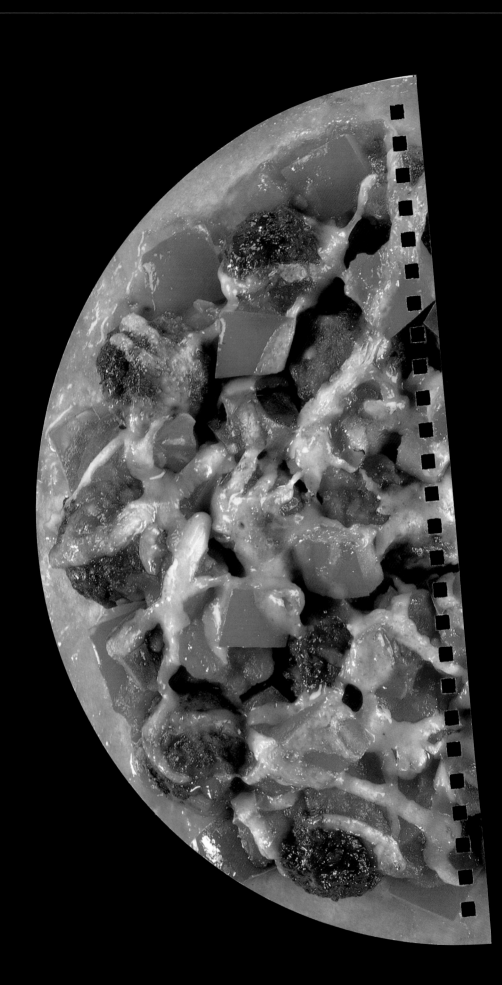

American-style Spicy Beef Pizza

The Americans have almost claimed pizzas as their own! They have certainly added some excellent meat toppings, spiced with chillies, to the traditional range. Add a chopped fresh chilli for extra heat!

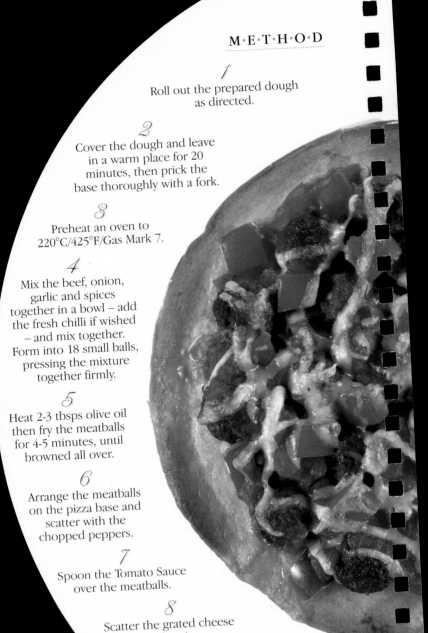

M·E·T·H·O·D

1
Roll out the prepared dough as directed.

2
Cover the dough and leave in a warm place for 20 minutes, then prick the base thoroughly with a fork.

3
Preheat an oven to 220°C/425°F/Gas Mark 7.

4
Mix the beef, onion, garlic and spices together in a bowl – add the fresh chilli if wished – and mix together. Form into 18 small balls, pressing the mixture together firmly.

5
Heat 2-3 tbsps olive oil then fry the meatballs for 4-5 minutes, until browned all over.

6
Arrange the meatballs on the pizza base and scatter with the chopped peppers.

7
Spoon the Tomato Sauce over the meatballs.

8
Scatter the grated cheese over the pizza.

9
Bake in the preheated oven for 20-25 minutes, until the base is cooked and the topping lightly browned.

American-style Spicy Beef Pizza

I·N·G·R·E·D·I·E·N·T·S

1 quantity Pizza Dough of your choice

175g/6oz lean minced beef

1 small onion, finely chopped

1 clove garlic, crushed

1 tsp ground allspice

1 tsp chilli powder

1 green chilli, chopped

2-3 tbsps olive oil

½ red pepper, seeded and chopped

½ green pepper, seeded and chopped

1 quantity Tomato Sauce

90g/3oz Cheddar cheese, grated

MAKES one 25cm/10-inch pizza
PREPARATION TIME: 40 minutes
COOKING TIME: 20-25 minutes

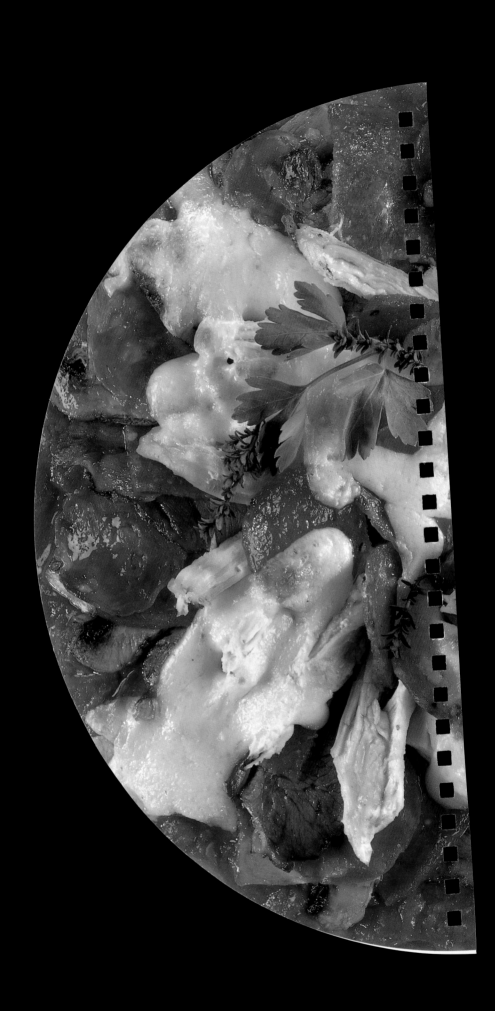

Meat Feast

A carnivore's delight! Use left-over cooked meats such as chicken or lamb, spicy sausages or a mixture of both. Include at least one slice of garlic sausage or salami.

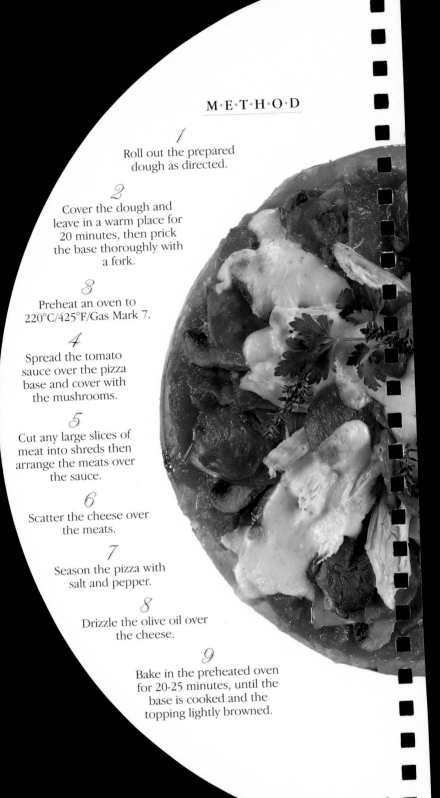

M·E·T·H·O·D

1

Roll out the prepared
dough as directed.

2

Cover the dough and
leave in a warm place for
20 minutes, then prick
the base thoroughly with
a fork.

3

Preheat an oven to
220°C/425°F/Gas Mark 7.

4

Spread the tomato
sauce over the pizza
base and cover with
the mushrooms.

5

Cut any large slices of
meat into shreds then
arrange the meats over
the sauce.

6

Scatter the cheese over
the meats.

7

Season the pizza with
salt and pepper.

8

Drizzle the olive oil over
the cheese.

9

Bake in the preheated oven
for 20-25 minutes, until the
base is cooked and the
topping lightly browned.

Meat Feast

I·N·G·R·E·D·I·E·N·T·S

1 quantity Pizza Dough of
your choice

1 quantity Tomato Sauce

60g/2oz mushrooms,
sliced

120g/4oz cooked or
smoked meats, sliced or
shredded

60g/2oz Mozzarella
cheese, grated

Salt and freshly ground
black pepper

1 tbsp olive oil

MAKES: one 25cm/10-inch
pizza
PREPARATION TIME: 25 minutes
COOKING TIME: 20-25 minutes

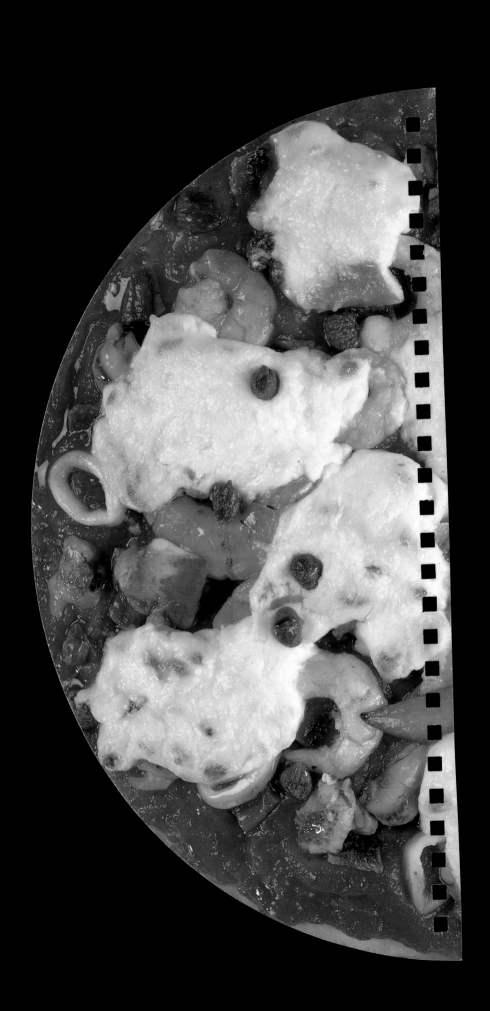

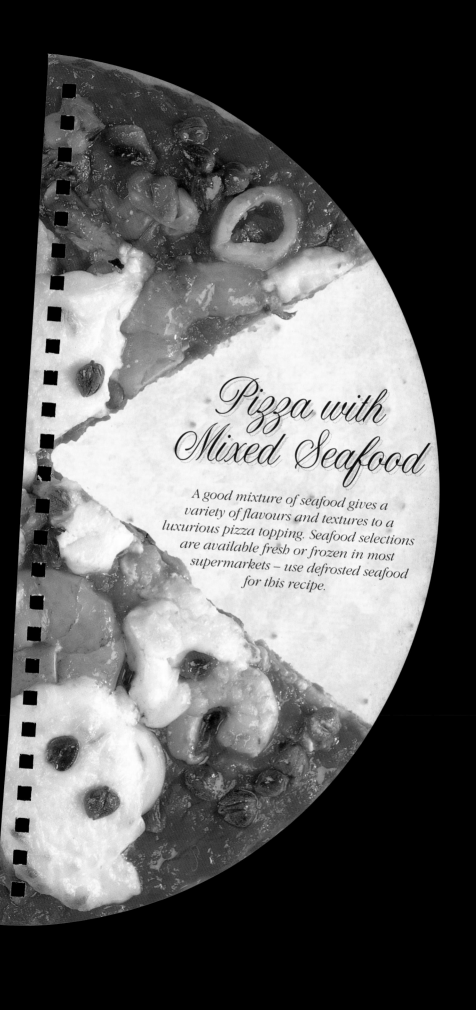

Pizza with Mixed Seafood

A good mixture of seafood gives a variety of flavours and textures to a luxurious pizza topping. Seafood selections are available fresh or frozen in most supermarkets – use defrosted seafood for this recipe.

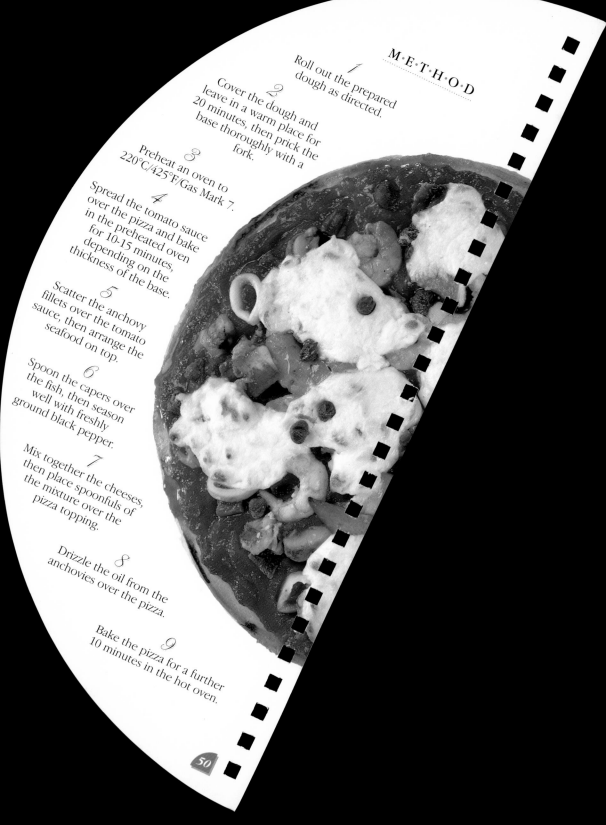

M·E·T·H·O·D

1
Roll out the prepared dough as directed.

2
Cover the dough and leave in a warm place for 20 minutes, then prick the base thoroughly with a fork.

3
Preheat an oven to 220°C/425°F/Gas Mark 7.

4
Spread the tomato sauce over the pizza and bake in the preheated oven for 10-15 minutes, depending on the thickness of the base.

5
Scatter the anchovy fillets over the tomato sauce, then arrange the seafood on top.

6
Spoon the capers over the fish, then season well with freshly ground black pepper.

7
Mix together the cheeses, then place spoonfuls of the mixture over the pizza topping.

8
Drizzle the oil from the anchovies over the pizza.

9
Bake the pizza for a further 10 minutes in the hot oven.

Pizza with Mixed Seafood

I·N·G·R·E·D·I·E·N·T·S

1 quantity Pizza Dough of your choice

1 quantity Tomato Sauce

50g/2oz can anchovy fillets, chopped

175g/6oz mixed seafood, eg prawns, mussels, squid etc

2 tsps capers

Freshly ground black pepper

60g/2oz Bel Paese cheese

60g/2oz full-fat cream cheese

MAKES: one 25cm/10-inch pizza
PREPARATION TIME: 30 minutes
COOKING TIME: 20-25 minutes

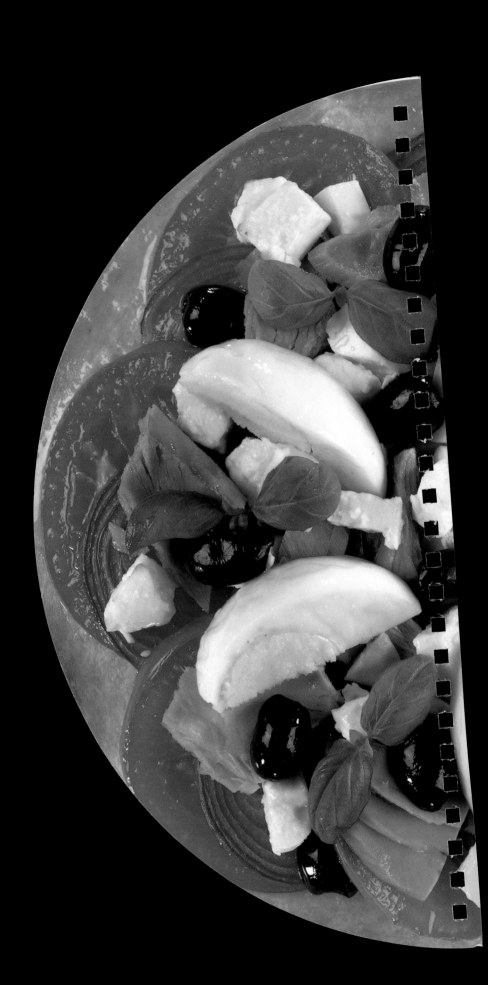

Tasty Tuna Pizza

Tuna pizzas can be surprising dull in flavour, but the addition of Feta cheese makes a really tasty topping. Add a tablespoon of capers with the olives if you like them.

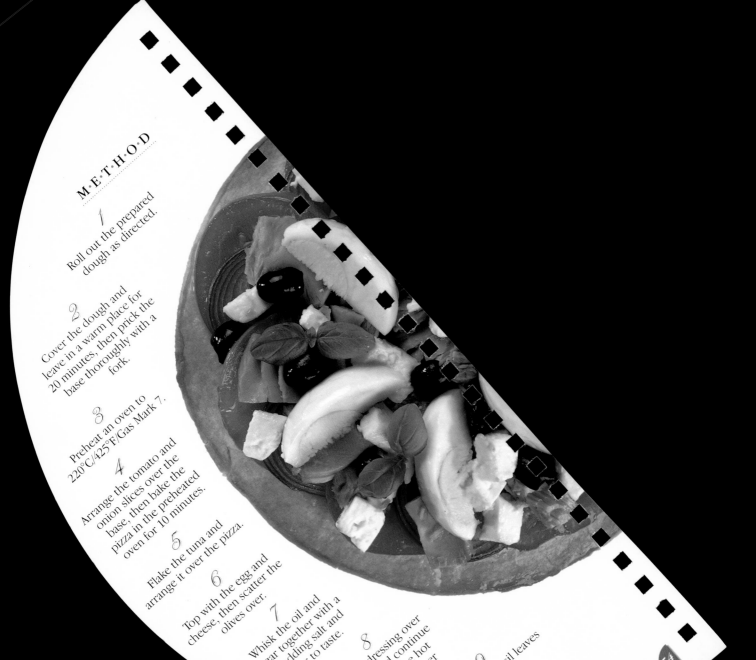

M·E·T·H·O·D

1

Roll out the prepared dough as directed.

2

Cover the dough and leave in a warm place for 20 minutes, then prick the base thoroughly with a fork.

3

Preheat an oven to 220°C/425°F/Gas Mark 7.

4

Arrange the tomato and onion slices over the base, then bake the pizza in the preheated oven for 10 minutes.

5

Flake the tuna and arrange it over the pizza.

6

Top with the egg and cheese, then scatter the olives over.

7

Whisk the oil and vinegar together with a little adding salt and to taste.

8

dressing over continue hot

il leaves

Tasty Tuna Pizza

I·N·G·R·E·D·I·E·N·T·S

1 quantity Pizza Dough of your choice

2 beef tomatoes, sliced

1 red onion, sliced

175g can tuna, drained

1 hard boiled egg, cut into wedges

120g/4oz Feta cheese, crumbled or sliced

8 black olives, pitted

3 tbsps olive oil

1 tbsp white wine vinegar

Salt and freshly ground black pepper

Fresh basil leaves, to garnish

MAKES one 25cm/10-inch pizza
PREPARATION TIME: 30 minutes
COOKING TIME: 20-25 minutes

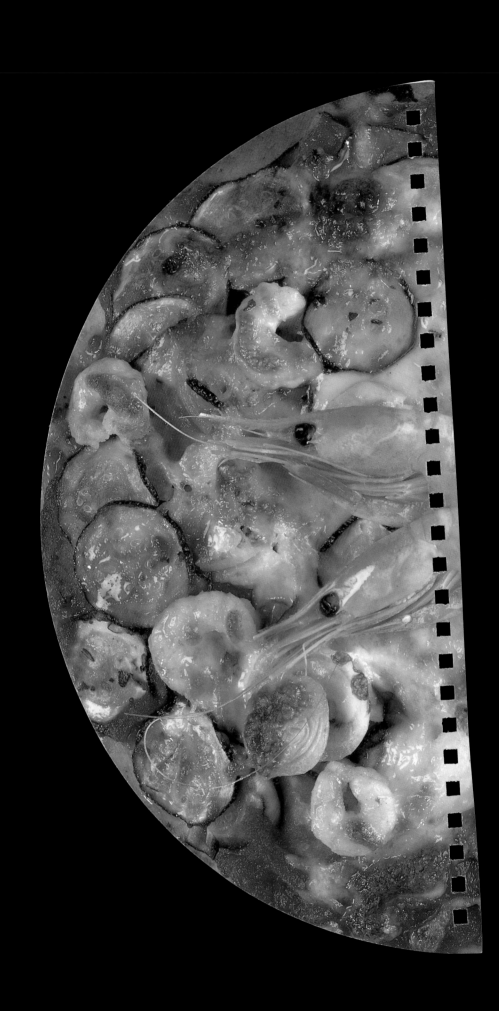

Fish Provençal Pizza

Prawns are often served in a herby tomato sauce.
This makes a delicious but expensive pizza,
so mix the prawns with cod or coley for
a more economical topping.

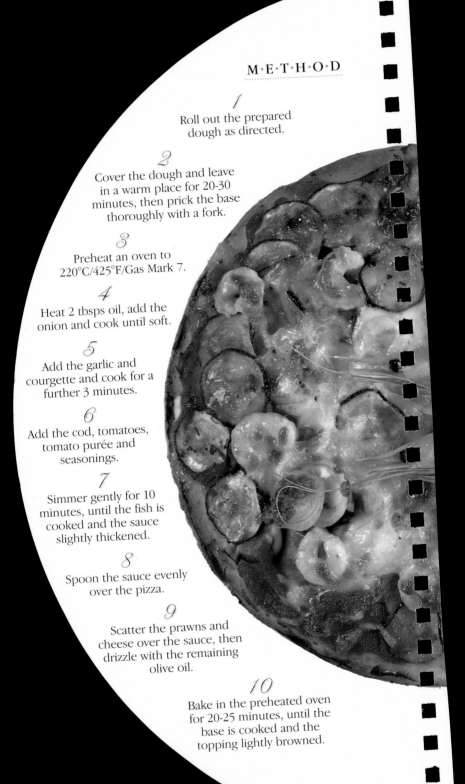

M·E·T·H·O·D

1
Roll out the prepared dough as directed.

2
Cover the dough and leave in a warm place for 20-30 minutes, then prick the base thoroughly with a fork.

3
Preheat an oven to 220°C/425°F/Gas Mark 7.

4
Heat 2 tbsps oil, add the onion and cook until soft.

5
Add the garlic and courgette and cook for a further 3 minutes.

6
Add the cod, tomatoes, tomato purée and seasonings.

7
Simmer gently for 10 minutes, until the fish is cooked and the sauce slightly thickened.

8
Spoon the sauce evenly over the pizza.

9
Scatter the prawns and cheese over the sauce, then drizzle with the remaining olive oil.

10
Bake in the preheated oven for 20-25 minutes, until the base is cooked and the topping lightly browned.

Fish Provençal Pizza

I·N·G·R·E·D·I·E·N·T·S

1 quantity Pizza Dough of your choice

3 tbsps olive oil

1 small onion, sliced

1 clove garlic, crushed

1 medium courgette, thinly sliced

120-150g/4-5oz cod or other white fish fillet, skinned and cubed

200g can chopped tomatoes

1 tbsp tomato purée

½ tsp dried herbes de Provençe

Salt and freshly ground black pepper

90g/3oz cooked peeled prawns

90g/3oz Mozzarella cheese, grated

MAKES one 25cm/10-inch pizza
PREPARATION TIME: 40 minutes
COOKING TIME: 20-25 minutes

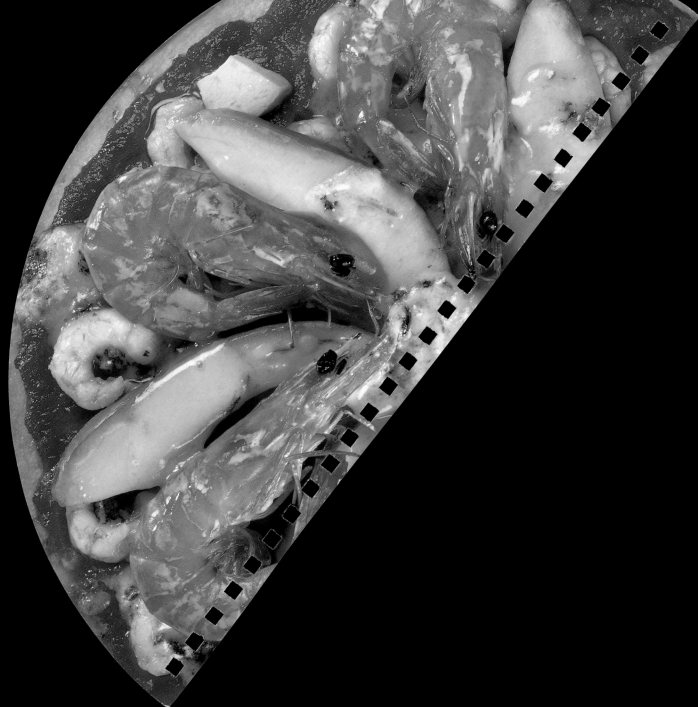

Prawn & Avocado Pizza

Hot avocado is delicious and makes a perfect partner for prawns. Use a blue cheese as an alternative to Mozzarella – Gorgonzola, Stilton, Shropshire Blue or Danish Blue will all work well.

M·E·T·H·O·D

1

Roll out the prepared
dough as directed.

2

Cover the dough and leave
in a warm place for 20
minutes, then prick the
base thoroughly with a fork.

3

Preheat an oven to
220°C/425°F/Gas Mark 7.

4

Spread the Tomato
Sauce evenly over the
pizza base, then bake in
the preheated oven for
10 minutes.

5

Cut the avocado in half
and remove the stone.
Peel, then slice one half
and chop the other. Toss
the avocado in lemon
juice to prevent
browning.

6

Scatter the chopped
avocado and peeled
prawns over the pizza.

7

Top with the sliced
avocado then the grated
cheese and arrange the
remaining prawns on top.

8

Season the pizza with salt
and pepper then drizzle
with the olive oil.

9

Bake in the preheated oven
for 20-25 minutes, until the
base is cooked and the
topping lightly browned.

Prawn & Avocado Pizza

I·N·G·R·E·D·I·E·N·T·S

1 quantity Pizza Dough of your choice

1 quantity Tomato Sauce

1 ripe avocado

Juice of half a lemon

120g/4oz cooked peeled prawns

90g/3oz Mozzarella or blue cheese, grated or crumbled

6 large unpeeled prawns

Salt and freshly ground black pepper

1 tbsp olive oil

Makes: one 25cm/10-inch pizza

Preparation Time: 30 minutes

Cooking Time: 20-25 minutes

Sweet Pepper & Sun-Dried Tomato Pizza

Use red, yellow and green peppers to make a bright, colourful pizza. The sun-dried tomatoes add a rustic flavour and the use of Ricotta cheese allows the vegetables to dominate this topping.

M·E·T·H·O·D

1

Preheat the oven to
220°C/425°F/Gas Mark 7.

2

Place the peppers on a
baking sheet and cook for
20-25 minutes, until blackened
and blistered. Turn the peppers
once during cooking.

3

Cover the peppers with a
damp cloth and leave to cool.

4

Roll out the prepared
dough as directed.

5

Cover the dough and
leave in a warm place for
20 minutes whilst
finishing the topping.

6

Skin the peppers – start
at the flower end and
pull off the skins towards
the stalk. Remove the
core and seeds and
roughly chop the flesh.

7

Arrange the peppers
over the pizza base and
top with the sun-dried
tomatoes and few torn
basil leaves.

8

Place teaspoonfuls of
cheese over the pizza, then
season well with salt and
pepper. Drizzle the oil
over the pizza.

9

Bake in the preheated oven
for 20-25 minutes, until the
base is cooked and the
topping lightly browned.

Sweet Pepper & Sun-Dried Tomato Pizza

I·N·G·R·E·D·I·E·N·T·S

1 red pepper

1 yellow pepper

1 green pepper

1 quantity Pizza Dough of your choice

2 tbsps olive oil

6 halves sun-dried tomatoes in oil, roughly chopped

Fresh basil leaves

90g/3oz Ricotta cheese

Salt and freshly ground black pepper

MAKES one 25cm/10-inch pizza
PREPARATION TIME: 30 minutes
COOKING TIME: 20-25 minutes

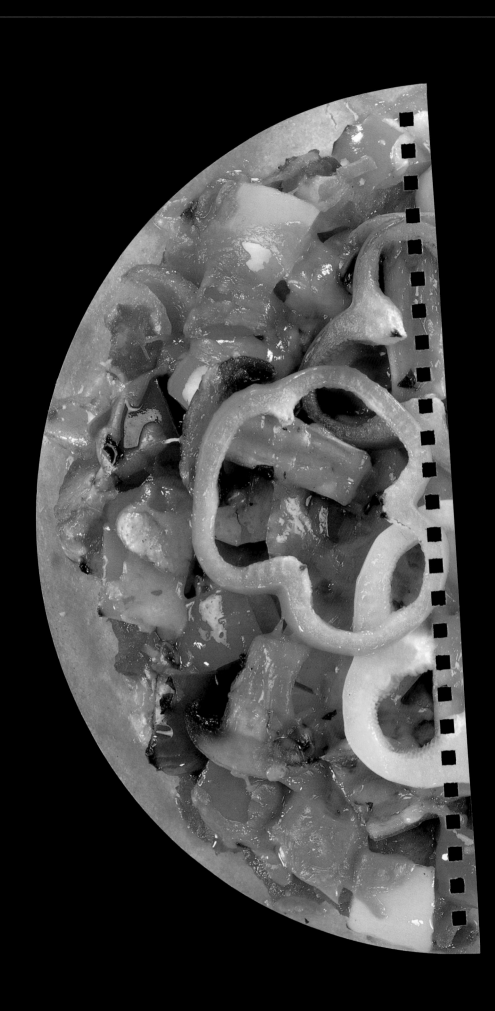

Spicy Vegetarian Pizza

The spice comes from chillies and Tabasco Sauce – use just one chilli for a milder flavour. Light-weight rubber gloves will protect your hands while preparing the chillies.

3
Preheat an oven to 220°C/
425°F/Gas Mark 7.

4
Heat 2 tbsps oil, add the
onion, garlic and chillies
and cook slowly for 5
minutes until softened.

5
Add the tomatoes and
Tabasco. Bring to the boil
then simmer gently for
15 minutes, until
thickened. Season to taste.

6
Slice two rings from
each pepper then chop
the remaining flesh.

7
Heat the remaining oil
and cook the chopped
peppers for 2 minutes.
Add the mushrooms and
cook for a further
3 minutes until soft.

8
Spread the tomato sauce over
the pizza base then top with
the peppers and mushrooms.

9
Mix the herbs with the cheeses and
scatter them over the pizza. Top with
the pepper rings, brushing them
with a little extra oil.

10
Bake in the preheated oven for
20-25 minutes, until the base is
cooked and the topping lightly
browned.

Spicy Vegetarian Pizza

I·N·G·R·E·D·I·E·N·T·S

1 quantity Pizza Dough of your choice

3 tbsps olive oil

1 large onion, chopped

2 cloves garlic, crushed

1 red chilli, seeded and chopped

1 green chilli, seeded and chopped

400g can chopped tomatoes

Few drops Tabasco Sauce

Salt and freshly ground black pepper

1/2 red pepper, seeded

1/2 green pepper, seeded

1/2 yellow pepper, seeded

90g/3oz mushrooms, sliced

1 tsp freshly chopped marjoram or oregano

60g/2oz Cheddar cheese, grated

60g/2oz Red Leicester cheese, grated

MAKES one 25cm/10-inch pizza
PREPARATION TIME: 45 minutes
COOKING TIME: 20-25 minutes

71

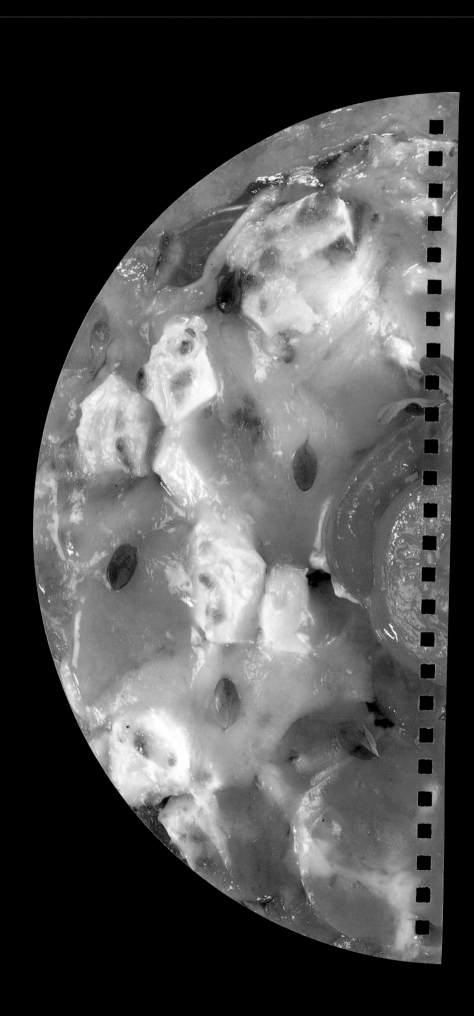

Pizza with Four Cheeses

Try to use four Italian cheeses for this classic vegetarian pizza – all those mentioned here are available in most large supermarkets or delicatessens. Plum tomatoes add a true Italian flavour.

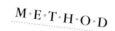

M·E·T·H·O·D

1

Roll out the prepared dough as directed.

2

Cover the dough and leave in a warm place for 20 minutes, then prick the base thoroughly with a fork.

3

Preheat an oven to 220°C/425°F/Gas Mark 7.

4

Spread the Tomato Sauce over the pizza base then top with the sliced tomatoes.

5

Bake in the preheated oven for 10 minutes.

6

Arrange the cheeses on the partially cooked pizza, either separately in quarters or mixing them all together.

7

Season with black pepper and drizzle with the olive oil.

8

Return the pizza to the hot oven for a further 10-15 minutes, until the cheeses have melted.

9

Garnish with fresh marjoram leaves before serving.

Pizza with Four Cheeses

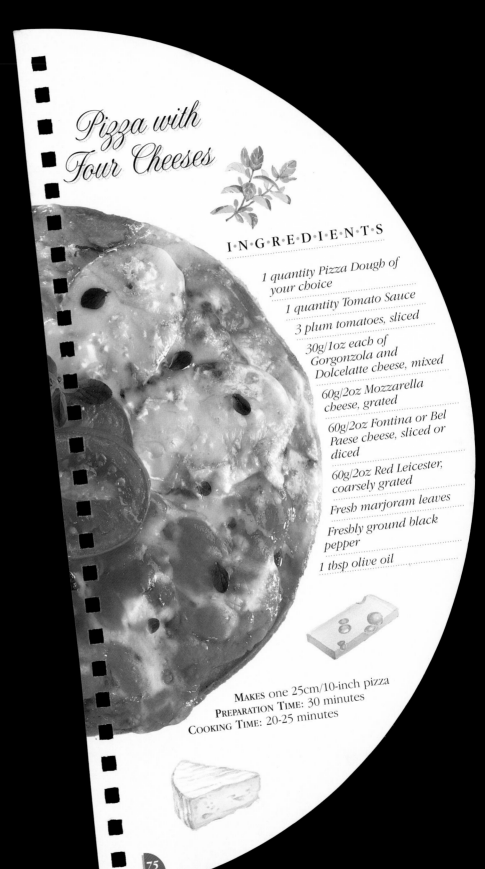

I·N·G·R·E·D·I·E·N·T·S

1 quantity Pizza Dough of your choice

1 quantity Tomato Sauce

3 plum tomatoes, sliced

30g/1oz each of Gorgonzola and Dolcelatte cheese, mixed

60g/2oz Mozzarella cheese, grated

60g/2oz Fontina or Bel Paese cheese, sliced or diced

60g/2oz Red Leicester, coarsely grated

Fresh marjoram leaves

Freshly ground black pepper

1 tbsp olive oil

MAKES one 25cm/10-inch pizza
PREPARATION TIME: 30 minutes
COOKING TIME: 20-25 minutes

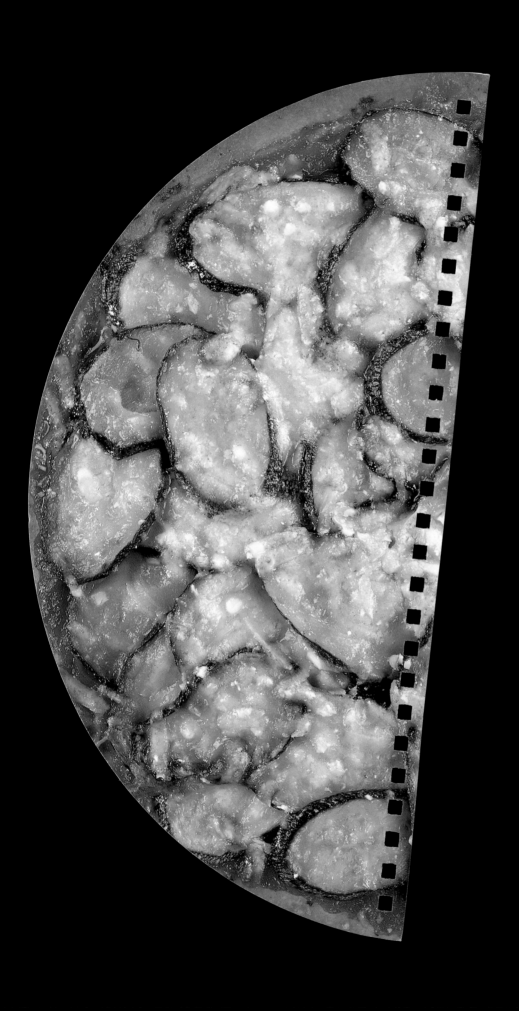

Courgette & Garlic Pizza

Cooking courgettes with garlic really emphasises their flavour. If you find Parmesan rather strong, use grated Mozzarella for the topping with just a little Parmesan scattered over the top.

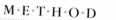

M·E·T·H·O·D

1
Roll out the prepared
dough as directed.

2
Cover the dough and leave
in a warm place for 20
minutes, then prick the
base thoroughly with a fork.

3
Preheat an oven to
220°C/425°F/Gas Mark 7.

4
Spread the Tomato Sauce
over the pizza base.

5
Heat 3 tbsps of oil and
cook the garlic until just
starting to brown. Add the
courgettes with the
oregano and continue
cooking until the
courgettes are lightly
browned on both sides –
add a little extra oil if
necessary.

6
Arrange the courgettes
and garlic over the
Tomato Sauce.

7
Season well with salt
and pepper.

8
Top with the grated Parmesan
then drizzle the remaining
oil over the pizza.

9
Bake in the preheated oven
for 20-25 minutes, until the
base is cooked and the
topping lightly browned.

Courgette & Garlic Pizza

I·N·G·R·E·D·I·E·N·T·S

1 quantity Pizza Dough of your choice

1 quantity Tomato Sauce

4 tbsps olive oil

4 cloves garlic, roughly chopped

4 small courgettes, 2 green and 2 yellow if possible, sliced

2 tsps freshly chopped oregano

Salt and freshly ground black pepper

60g/2oz Parmesan cheese, freshly grated

MAKES one 25cm/10-inch pizza
PREPARATION TIME: 40 minutes
COOKING TIME: 20-25 minutes

Index